The Forever Tree

Hilary Hawkes

"Books are the quietest and most constant of friends; they are the most accessible and wisest of counselors, and the most patient of teachers."

Charles William Eliot (1834-1926), The Happy Life, 1896, USA

THE FOREVER TREE

Words © Hilary Hawkes 2015

Front cover, small tree on back cover and interior images: Pixabay.com according to their usage agreement

Four seasons tree picture on back cover and inside, credit: DeepGreen/Shutterstock.com

First print edition by Strawberry Jam Books 2015

British Library Cataloguing in Publication Data

A CIP catalogue record for this book is available from the British Library

Abingdon-on-Thames, UK

www.hilaryhawkes.co.uk/strawberryjambooks

ISBN 978-1-910257-17-3

Welcome to the place of The Forever Tree!

Imagine a warm and sunny place to walk with a
winding path for you to run or stroll along!

Imagine!

Can you see the tall tree at the
side of the path?

Its branches are strong and
stretch up and out all around.

Pretend you are a
tree like that!

How would it feel to be
a tree?
Look up and spread out your
arms – wiggle your fingers.
Your arms are the branches
and your fingers are
the leaves.

Imagine the blue sky above and
the warm sun!

Stand tall. Feel the ground
beneath your feet. You're as tall
and strong as the tree trunk.
Wriggle your toes – they are the
roots keeping you safe and
attached to the soil.

Summer!

It's summer!
The sun is bright. White
clouds drift across the sky.
Your branches are full and
heavy with flowers and
amazing green leaves.

They rustle in the gentle
breeze.

You feel warm and
happy and good.

You remember your roots holding you firmly in the ground.

Autumn!

Autumn comes!

The wind is cooler and the sun is weaker.

Your leaves get tired and drop one by one.

When the wind blows stronger, or the rain falls and you shake your branches, more leaves shower down to the ground.

Your leaves have turned from green to red, brown and yellow.

Your roots feel the moisture in the soil. And they hold you firm and strong.

Winter!

Now it is winter.

You have no leaves left! Your branches

are bare and spiky. How do they feel?

You are buffeted and hit by the storms.

Snow lands on your branches and

covers you like icing.

In the frozen soil your roots hold you strong and safe.

The sun comes back
and you feel warm again.

You stretch your branches. They are refreshed from the winter cold. New leaves and blossom appear. You notice you are bigger than you once were!

All through the summer, all through the autumn, all through the winter and back to spring, your roots held you strong and safe.

Spring! Whatever season happens, it passes away again and there you are still: a beautiful and perfect tree.

A Forever Tree.

Sad things can happen. Difficult things can happen.

Good and exciting things can happen – just like the seasons, everything comes and goes.

You are not the seasons. Just like the Forever Tree, you can stand tall and safe through all the seasons.

Forever You.

Whatever season happens, it passes away again.

And there you are still. A beautiful and perfect tree.

How to share, use and discus the Forever Tree image with a child

Photocopy and cut out the leaves and star from page three of this book.

Open the book at the double page that shows the tree with four seasons. Place the picture of this tree in front of you. Place the star in the middle of the tree. Imagine the star is part of the strong tree which is held safe by the strong roots. Imagine you are the star.

Decide which season it is: what season does life feel like right now? Maybe lots of things are changing and it feels like autumn where everything changes or some things end.

Maybe something sad or difficult is happening for you and perhaps you feel worried or unhappy. So maybe that feels like winter.

Maybe new things are beginning and that feels exciting and hopeful like spring. Or maybe you feel great! Perhaps it's summer right now!

Place some of the leaves on the tree. Put different colours in different seasons, except for winter which has no leaves. Flick the leaves down to the ground at the bottom of the picture and place some new leaves on the tree in a different season.

Talk together about how the leaves and the seasons are all the things that happen in life. Remember you're not the seasons, or the leaves or the weather. The seasons come and go and everything that happens changes in time. You are like the star and Forever Tree: Forever You!

Sadness

Sometimes things happen that make us sad.

Choose a leaf to be the sad happening and place it on the tree.

How does the sad leaf feel?

What does it want to say?

Place the star in the middle of the tree. You are the star that sits in the middle of the tree which has roots that keep it standing strong and tall.

What can you say to the sad leaf?

Imagine the wind blowing, the sun shining.

Place some more leaves on the tree so that the sad leaf is one of many leaves. Not all the leaves are sad leaves!

Now imagine the leaves blowing down to the ground. You can push the leaves to the bottom of the picture.

Talk about how sad things can come and go and that they are a part of life.

Notice that the star hasn't moved or changed – only the leaves and the seasons or weather. Whatever happens the part of you that is really you remains the same – just like the star and just like the Forever Tree.

Worries

Choose a leaf to be the worry. You could put lots of leaves close together or on top of each other for a big worry.

Listen to what the worry leaves want to say. Sometimes worries exaggerate to get us all worked up and worry even more. They also like to convince us that they can predict the future or know for sure what will happen.

Place the star in the centre of the picture. Remember you are the star, you're not the worry leaves.

Imagine the calm and peaceful star talking to the worry – what does it say? Can it tell when the worries are exaggerating to trying to make you feel worse than things might be?

Remember you are the star and not the worries. You are in charge of the worries and can get them to calm down!

Notice all the other things in the picture. There is more there than the worries. Imagine the wind blowing and the seasons changing.

Everything changes and moves on in time. Push the worry leaves to the bottom of the picture. Talk together about how life is like seasons that come and go around us. But we are not the seasons.

Who we are inside remains safe and strong like the star in the middle of the Forever Tree.

Happiness

What things make you happy? Choose some leaves to be those happy things and place them on the tree.

How does everything look and feel when you are happy?

If the happy leaves could talk what would they be saying?

Does everyone and everything stay happy all the time?

Place the star in the middle of the tree and pretend you are the star which is part of the tree. Remember the tree has roots that keep it strong and safe in the ground.

The star is always peaceful and calm.

Happy things happen, sad things can happen, but you can remember that you are always like the calm and peaceful star.

Whatever happens, the part of you that is really you remains the same – just like the star and just like the Forever Tree.

Other books in the award winning Story Therapy series include:

Just Be with Bizzy Bee

Stories for Feelings for children – illustrated and non-illustrated editions.

And see www.hilaryhawkes.co.uk/strawberryjambooks

16251131R00015

Printed in Great Britain
by Amazon